Finding Our Way

Proceeds from the sale of this book will support the work of two charities:

Mission Aviation Fellowship flies small aircraft bringing medicine, education and the good news of God's love in Jesus to some of the world's most remote locations. More information is available on their website: www.maf.org

A21 seeks to help the victims and tackle the global issue of human trafficking and modern-day slavery. More information is available on their website: www.a21.org

Finding
Our Way
HOME

Prayers and
Reflections
for Our Journey
in Christ

ANDREW WATSON

VERITAS

Published 2016 by Veritas Publications
7–8 Lower Abbey Street
Dublin 1, Ireland
publications@veritas.ie
www.veritas.ie

ISBN 978 1 84730 764 4

Copyright © Andrew Watson, 2016

10 9 8 7 6 5 4 3 2 1

The material in this publication is protected by copyright law.
Except as may be permitted by law, no part of the material may be
reproduced (including by storage in a retrieval system) or transmitted
in any form or by any means, adapted, rented or lent without
the written permission of the copyright owners. Applications for
permissions should be addressed to the publisher.

A catalogue record for this book is available from the British Library.

Cover designed by Heather Costello, Veritas Publications
Printed in the Republic of Ireland by Walsh Colour Print, Kerry

*Veritas books are printed on paper made from the wood pulp of managed forests.
For every tree felled, at least one tree is planted, thereby renewing natural
resources.*

Dedication

To Hazel –
my sweet helper, most loyal critic and lifelong best friend,
and to our wonderful no-longer-kids, Michael, Joshua,
Sarah and Emily –
you guys are our greatest adventure!

Contents

Welcome!

Praying is natural.

We see a beautiful sunrise and instinctively want to praise and thank someone or something for the hope born in a new day.

We foul up, some careless word or selfish, dishonourable deed and we need someone to hear our confession.

We face the ridiculous challenge of living in a world where opportunity seems finely balanced with the human tendency to self-destruct. Who feels adequate for the task? We need help from beyond ourselves.

The Christian 'Good News' is that there is an Almighty Creator, deeply concerned and passionately involved in this world, to the extent He became part of it in Jesus. He loves us. He came to our rescue. And He would like to hear from us. 'Our Father in Heaven' welcomes his children when we pray!

I grew up knowing and believing this. I'm profoundly grateful to my mum Dorothy and late dad John who kept the promises they made at my Baptism and faithfully knelt by my bedside to teach me my first childhood prayers. As an ordained church minister I regularly lead others in prayer and have been deeply blessed by people praying with and for me.

I can't remember many days in my life when I haven't prayed. But sometimes I feel I'm not very good at it.

My mind is not as disciplined as it might be. I forget things. At other times I really care about things but honestly am not sure *how* to pray about them. That's where I found the liturgies and prayer books of other traditions helpful.

So this book began as a few clumsy attempts to write in words what I try to communicate when I open my mind and heart to speak with the Lord and Master in whom I trust.

How liberating a journey it has been!

Initially I thought I might have written seven prayers, one for each day of the week, but the number kept growing. I'm grateful to Veritas who suggested supplementing the prayers with the kind of biblical 'Thoughts' I write weekly on my website wordsurfers.com.

I hope the result is an encouraging combination of honest, poignant, sometimes funny but, above all, Christ-honouring writings that will help you on your journey of growing faith with the Lord. He is, after all, 'the Lord *our Shepherd*'.

May he guide us all safely home!

A Touch

A snowflake touched my lips today
As I walked in the street, unprepared.
One single, crystalline miracle fell,
Helplessly colliding with me, awakened
Now to see and think and dream.

Is random beauty a cold, sharp shock
To tease then mock us, mid-path;
Or some guided missile of love, sent
To make us believe again? The warmth
Of my heart today must decide.

Home

Some people are blessed to have a 'homeplace' where their family have been for generations. Others don't.

I was counting up and think I have lived in at least ten different places during my lifetime. It's not uncommon these days. Families grow up and often move away for education or employment. Other people live in the houses where we played as children. The church meeting house in Belfast where I was baptised as an infant was knocked down many years ago. In Agnes Street nowadays not one building remains that was there when I was a child.

I'm reminded of an old vinyl record by Jim Reeves my Mum used to play:

'This world is not my home, I'm just a-passing through.
My treasures are laid up somewhere beyond the blue.'

It's not that I'm complaining! Most of the places I've lived in have been really nice. As the Bible puts it, 'the boundary lines have fallen for me in pleasant places' (Psalm 16:6).

But I guess 'home' is more than just familiar surroundings and a few creature comforts – it's about belonging and being secure among people you love. 'Home' can be anywhere when we know we are accepted, valued and, when necessary, forgiven.

Moses was reared in the royal palace in Egypt but always knew he didn't belong. He left to wander as a shepherd in Midian, then wandered for a further forty years leading the rebellious Israelites to their Promised Land. Even then, he

12

didn't get to own property or build a house, but died before crossing the Jordan river.

Was he disappointed? I don't think so. Reflecting on life in Psalm 90 he writes: 'Lord, you have been our dwelling-place throughout all generations.'

His relationship with God had proved the greatest source of comfort and security through the changing circumstances of his life. It's a lesson worth learning. Grateful as we are for our homes on Earth, however nice they are, we should recognise that they are temporary.

We find our ultimate 'homeplace' only when we learn to trust in the grace and provision of the One who is 'from everlasting to everlasting'.

For then we shall 'rest in the shadow of the Almighty' (Psalm 91:1) and can look forward to dwelling 'in the house of the Lord forever' (Psalm 23:6).

Family Prayer

Father in Heaven, my family and me, we're far from perfect, but thank you anyway.

Thank you for each other and for the unique bond that makes us 'us'.

For the brilliant times we've shared, when we laughed till we almost cried.

And for the times we *have* cried in pain, the proof that we really care.

Lord, thank you for your generous love.

For your faithful, patient hanging in with us when we feel so unsure about things.

For your giving of yourself that we might know forgiveness and this glorious possibility –

Of sharing love in your family always.

So Lord, please accept this prayer, for parents, partners, children, siblings,

And those whose loyal friendship makes them a family to us:

For grace to trust and follow you, your spirit within and among all,

For wisdom in the wilderness,

Courage in the storms,

And the desire to show kindness in our everyday living.

May your peace protect our minds and hearts, and help us all to be a blessing,

In your name.

Amen.

Bringing Little Ones for Baptism

Lord, you have graciously saved and blessed us.
Please save and bless our children
Whom we identify with you today
With this 'Jesus picture' we call Baptism.
As you have forgiven and renewed us by your Spirit,
Cleanse and give new life to these dear ones.
Include them in your covenant of love!

From earliest days may they sense your comforting, guiding presence,
And learn to trust and obey.
May they grow to love your Word and live in ways pleasing to you,
And be a blessing to those they meet.

Lord, they're so young.
They won't remember this day.
But we will, and you will.

So help us to practise the profession we make with genuine lifestyle,
And help us follow through on the serious promise we're making.
Show us ways to make our home and Church a place of love, and reverence, and joy!
Make us the example of faith and obedience they need.
Make the picture real for us all.

Oh, and... thank you! For grace, and for everything.
Amen.

A Picture of God

A small girl was drawing with crayons. Her teacher noticed her brow furrowed in concentration and asked her what she was drawing.

'I'm drawing a picture of God,' came the reply.

'That's nice,' said the teacher, 'although no one really knows what God looks like.'

'They will when I'm finished,' said the child.

Jesus loved little children. On the first Palm Sunday he chased the crooked traders from God's house and welcomed little children. Sure, they were noisy but they loved Jesus and trusted him implicitly. (cf. Matthew 21:15–16)

On another occasion he told his disciples they needed to 'convert', to be changed, to become more trusting like little children if they wanted to see and enter God's kingdom (cf. Matthew 18:1–4).

A childlike heart is open to miracles, open to love and open to God. In John 1:12 we're promised that, whatever age we are, to those who receive him and believe in his name, Jesus gives power to become 'children of God'.

So that, even if our best art really can't do him justice in the short term, we can look forward to one day seeing our Heavenly Father as he is, face to face.

And that will be glory.

For our Children

Lord, thank you for entrusting us with these precious young ones,
So alive, so fresh with individual personality, imagination, expression.
Thank you for the glorious, noisy, 'huggy' mess our home has become!
For the priceless opportunities to play on the floor again, read stories,
And experiment with a host of new hobbies.

We love them and are so proud of them.
How could we not desire and pray for all that is best for them?

Of course we ask for safety, good health and employment but ...
May we ask for more?
That you would love and guide and teach them with every new opportunity,
Growing in them good and wise and reverent hearts,
And joyful, thankful, fun, creative attitudes.

May they be kind and loving, and may they be loved.
Please bless them with faithful, lifelong partners,
Homes and families of their own.
May those as yet unborn, the generations as yet unnamed,
Live to know your goodness and mercy.

To that end, help us to be the loyal, encouraging, inspiring parents they need and deserve.
Amen.

Kitchen Prayer

Lord, you have provided me with this space, and a little time
to live here.
For shelter, a warm stove and our daily bread, I thank you.
Often the boundary lines have fallen for me in pleasant places,
And yet even in the wilderness you have been my refuge.

So Lord, I ask you to make me hospitable.
Give me a heart to share my roof and food with others,
generously.
May people find comfort, love and renewed faith at my table.
And please be assured that even as Abraham entertained you,
and your angels without knowing it,
You will always be my most honoured guest.
Help me to see your face when I welcome those in need
Of food, company or forgiveness.

Son of God, you who took on flesh to share our space here,
Growing up in a carpenter's house, camping with disciples or
enjoying dinner at your friends' homes in Bethany –
Pitch your tabernacle in my mind and heart,
Make my kitchen and my soul your home on earth for now.
Make my whole life a place of welcome in your name,
That I may be content and of service wherever I am,
Knowing I shall dwell in your house forever.
Amen.

Clean-up

You see it every year around March. The local crows start to nest. The daffodils come out, and in some of the fields you'll see lambs. Despite the breeze and stubborn last flurries of snow, Ireland is bravely trying to move into Spring. Each year, as an act of faith I leave my motorbike with a friend for servicing. I resolve to believe that it will get warmer and one of these days I'll get out for a spin.

I leave it into Willie's garage without a second thought, for two reasons. One, I know he's fair and won't charge me an arm and a leg. Two, I know he's absolutely meticulous and my old bike will emerge from that garage in better than showroom condition!

It kind of reminds me of Jesus. I bring to Him my heart and life, somewhat worn and battered as they are, and badly tarnished with sin. He welcomes me in, cleans and fixes me up, and gets me on the road again.

All he asks is that I humbly trust Him, like a young child (Mark 10:14,15).

An old children's hymn comes to mind:

'If I come to Jesus, He will hear my prayer.
He will love me dearly; He my sins did bear.
If I come to Jesus, happy shall I be.
He is gently calling little ones like me.'

In the Shed

Lord, this is my workshop, my store, my den, my retreat,
And you are welcome here.
It's where I keep tools, animal feed, fuel and fertiliser.
There's the lawnmower and the old tractor,
Near vintage now, like their owner!
Under that tarpaulin there's a wee 'restoration project'
I tinker with over the winter months.
And here's the bench, chipped and worn, where I work.
Sometimes it's noisy in here but you were probably used
to that in the carpentry shop in Nazareth.

It's just my shed Lord, but like everything else
I want it to somehow honour you.
May it be a place of useful labour,
And worthwhile recreation,
Of fellowship with mates,
And of time spent with you.
Yes Lord, be with me even out here!
Make this humble space a part of your kingdom,
And a house of prayer –
For my family, neighbours and friends,
For your glory.
Amen.

College Prayer

Lord, all around me there is a universe to discover,
With a billion things I still don't know or understand.
Thank you for every day, every opportunity to learn,
To grow in appreciation of all that you have done and do,
The complex genius of the scientific,
The exuberant celebration of the natural.

Thank you for eyes and ears and senses to experience,
And faculties to assess and reflect,
And a heart to love and brim with pleasure!

I ask your blessing on our places of learning,
On teachers and students both.
In our study, make us diligent.
In power, make us responsible.
In knowledge, make us humble,
Mindful of wisdom and authority far above ours.

As we expand in learning, help us grow in our souls,
That we might put our lessons and abilities to good use in the
world.
And help us remember always the Teacher who promised:
'The meek shall inherit the earth.'
And taught his students to pray, 'Our Father in heaven …'
Amen.

Getting Older

My child is suddenly grown and gone away.
His life's adventure continues across the sea,
And it's okay.
He sounds so happy on the phone and that's good.

I haven't gone into his bedroom yet, though the door is ajar.
I know it's strangely tidy and quiet in there,
All those games we tried together neatly stacked,
Shelves filled with memories, like our hearts.

Last year we did a charity run together and I wondered
About the little boy I used to carry piggyback,
Waiting for me now at the finish –
Did he get faster or have I just gotten slow?

He's grown up and is seizing life, capable and unafraid.
Good Man! I'm his dad, happy and proud,
Yet also, suddenly, I'm a child again,
Bereft, and wanting to cry out loud.

Wedding Prayer

Lord, be our Chief Guest today.
Witness our vows, hear our prayers, and smile your blessing
On this couple being joined in your name.

You know what it is to be human,
And how relationships can be hard work,
And how love can be sorrow as well as joy.

May these two be lovers all their days,
Happy and comfortable together
Sharing space, warmth, affection.
More, may they be one, a true partnership,
Their joy to help each other constantly,
As time brings new challenges and adventures.
And may they be lifelong best friends,
Talking and listening, laughing and weeping,
Through good and bad times, always faithful.

Help them to be patient, kind, trusting, persevering;
Not selfish, cruel, jealous or resentful.
Bless them with the love that never fails.
Amen.

Recreation Prayer

Lord, when you were finished working on creation, you chose to rest.
Lord of Sabbath, creator of 'free' time, origin of pleasure,
Thank you for times to rest, refresh and enjoy things!
May our recreation be pleasing to you!

Help us to choose positive interests
That we might be creative, like you.
Show us colourful, wholesome things with which
To fill our minds and employ our hands.
Help us balance our passion for the game with fair play.
Make our friendships sweet, our times together fun,
Be our guest when we eat, drink, laugh and sing.
Keep us from spoiling things
With over-indulgence, laziness or disrespect.
Remove jealousy and malice far from us.

And invite us to remember you, the Giver of good things,
And to set aside priority time for you.
Teach us to worship with thanksgiving,
To seek your presence and hear your Word
As our greatest pleasure.
Amen.

Work Prayer

Lord, in the beginning you delighted in what you had made,
you said it was good.
Creator God, I agree. I applaud the excellence of your work,
And would like to talk to you about mine.

Thank you for a measure of health, for the education I received,
And for the abilities you have given people to do useful things.
Thank you for opportunities for meaningful activity today,
For the dignity of earning our food and pleasure.

Help us, whatever we do, to conduct our business with
enthusiasm, integrity, and a responsible attitude towards
people and the environment.
When facing difficulty, make us wise, ingenious, dutiful and
persevering.

Help us to value those in our team, to treat them and members
of the public with courtesy, appreciation and respect.
When facing criticism, make us patient, constructive and
gracious in response.

Help us, in everything, to do an excellent job that will give
service and delight to the community and world.

And later may we rest from today's tasks, tired but content in
the knowledge
Of your pleasure, and never-failing grace.
Amen.

Unemployment Prayer

Lord, sometimes I feel useless, hopeless, redundant,
Like Joseph in an Egyptian dungeon, rejected, passed by, like
I'm a waste of space.
I'm bored and frustrated, somewhere between anger and
sorrow,
Resentful but also self-critical, bitter but needing loved.

But with you there are no hopeless cases,
No people beyond redeeming. I am trusting you,
But in my head and my heart I'm struggling and need help.

I choose to believe you have a worthwhile plan for my and
every life.
I choose to open my mind to your leading,
To study and learn new skills, to employ the abilities you give
me,
To do something positive and creative each day,
To make myself eager to serve my community.

I ask you to deliver me from the depression and negativity.
I ask you to make me useful, helpful, an asset anywhere.
I ask you to help me be flexible in my attitude
And show me new opportunities.

Grant this request – the honour of working and earning my
living,
That I might be able to provide for those I love,
And be able to support others in need.
In your name.
Amen.

Delete?

Some time ago I was invited back to my old parish to take part in a funeral service. It was an honour to speak of someone who had been vivacious and funny, conscientious about her work, a devoted family person and a kind friend to so many of us.

Some time afterwards I came across her number on my mobile and thought, with sadness, about how wouldn't be needing it again. But as I tried to remove the name the message came up on the screen, 'Cannot delete this contact'.

It was fitting in a way because family and friends we have known and loved can never be deleted from our hearts. While we entrust them to the grace and care of our Master in Heaven, they live on in another way, in our thoughts and memories. Always.

Several scripture passages come to mind:

Exiled giant-killer David, grieving over his friend and comrade Prince Jonathan. (cf. 2 Samuel 1:26)

Imprisoned church leader Paul, writing to thank his old parish in Philippi who had thought to send their former pastor some support. (cf. Philippians 4:14–20)

Not least God Himself, assuring His people in Jerusalem, 'I will not forget you. See, I have engraved you on the palms of my hands…' (cf. Isaiah 49:15–16).

Thanks be to God for his faithful, tender mercy, and for all those precious individuals who have in various ways touched and enriched our lives. Gone, but not deleted!

Friends

Dear Lord, thank you for these dear people,
This eclectic fellowship of 'rogues anonymous',
Loyal team mates, companions on the journey,
Who walk, dance or limp alongside me so willingly, without condemning;
Pals who share the pizza, the game, the music, tears and laughter,
Who remember and forget all the right things,
Who say what helps and swallow what doesn't,
Who seem to actually like my company,
Who let me be myself, who appreciate when I try to help,
And who always have my back –
My friends.

Sometimes they shine so wonderfully,
And sometimes they're a bit broken like me,
But they're my friends, and I'd like you to bless them.

Lord, remind us that you became human to befriend us all,
You laid down your life that we could be friends with the Almighty.
Help us to realise your realness and nearness, your desire for our trust,
And the struggling seeds of love and goodness that you're trying to grow in us,
Which I guess are reflected in our poor but precious attempts at relationship!

Thanks for your grace this far – I'm still trusting you
To forgive and hang in with us and make something really good of us –
Friends For Life, and eternity!
Amen.

The Hills of Donegal

North Donegal is almost ridiculously picturesque. Rugged beauty seems to lie in all directions.

Then there's the light. The way the sun sometimes breaks through to intensify the colours of sea and landscape, or comes through the cloud to give an almost ethereal effect.

Such beautiful scenery might make some people think of heaven, but I'm reminded of something the New Testament says:

'No eye has seen, no ear has heard, no mind has conceived what God has prepared for those who love Him.' (1 Corinthians 2:9)

In other words no matter how grand it is now, what is yet to come will be even more glorious! The most spectacular coastal sunset in this present fallen world will pale into insignificance when our risen Lord returns and our heavenly Father 'makes all things new'.

So Christians are people who are living in grateful anticipation. With thanks to our Lord who loves us and gave Himself for us, we live as those who are looking forward to meeting him face to face, and living forever in his beautiful light.

When We Must Say Goodbye

Lord, I need your help again, this time
To do what is probably the hardest thing I've ever had to do,
To consider and now face what I've always found unthinkable.
It seems that it is time to say goodbye,
Time to take leave of someone I care about very deeply.
My head tells me it is so, and yet my heart resists the inevitable.
I honestly don't want to do this. Please help me, us…

Thank you for the precious times we've been given to share,
The gifts of life and love to nurture and enjoy,
The privilege of laughing and crying our way through so much
together,
Becoming so much a part of each other, inseparable.

Except now you are separating us, at least for a while,
And I, we, need to know Lord, that you really do have us
covered,
Here, there, wherever!
That by your grace we are forgiven, accepted, rescued and
secure;
That the One who died and rose again is preparing a place,
And waiting to welcome all God's children there,
There, where these tears will be wiped away
And all will be made new.

So, help us rest now Lord, and when the time comes,
Part us with your blessing,
Help us to release each other into your care,
In faith, in hope and in never ending love.
Amen.

Prayer for Health

Lord I know we can't be happy and healthy all the time,
Not this side of heaven, not in a still-fallen, broken world.
But I believe in you and your ultimate grace,
In Jesus as my Saviour, the Son of God, and Lord of all,
Who died and rose triumphant to bring on your kingdom.
I believe in the forgiveness of sins, Resurrection and the life
everlasting!

So in anticipation of your perfect restoration to glory,
In the all-commanding name of Jesus,
I ask for a measure of health, wholeness and strength,
In my body and my soul, my mind and my emotions.
And I ask the same for those I name before you now,
That we might live this gift of life today with joy,
Serving one another and honouring you.

Lord, thank you for those called to practise medicine,
For doctors, nurses, paramedics, therapists, care workers,
All who provide help and comfort for our well-being here.
Grant to them insight and skill, patience and thoroughness,
And most of all compassion,
The heart of Christ towards the sick and bereaved.

Be close to us in times of weakness, loss or pain,
And when our time here is done, grant us courage to die well,
In faith, hope, gratitude, peace and never ending love.
Amen.

Liberation

The Gospels give us an account of the disciples of Jesus having difficulty driving out a demon. It was causing extreme physical symptoms in a young man. This should not have been a problem as their Master had delegated authority to them to do this kind of ministry, and they had done so effectively before. But on this occasion they seemed to be having extra difficulty. Jesus arrived, banished the evil spirit and the boy was healed.

What is intriguing is Jesus' answer when the disciples asked him about their failure. He replied, 'This kind can come out only by prayer.' (Mark 9:29)

So there are some things that are simply beyond us to do on our own, even with delegated authority. Some situations in life where we are basically helpless without higher power from beyond ourselves. Circumstances beyond our control. Family members causing anxiety. Addictions too strong to break. Poverty. Terrorism. War.

There are occasions, perhaps far more than we would realise or admit, when we need to earnestly cry out for help to Almighty God for his grace and help. There's no shame in this. The Bible calls it praying. The disciples noticed Jesus doing it. A lot.

We may feel powerless to change the world, but we make a significant contribution to it all when we pray, and surrender our hearts, minds, lives to God to heal and change us.

Evil can try and make harmful, binding inroads in our lives through very natural human feelings like bitterness and anger but thanks be to God: he gives us freedom and victory through our Lord Jesus Christ!

Freedom Prayer

Lord, there are many things that seek to keep me bound –
People and devils, systems, rules and restrictions,
Money, barbed wire, promises and threats.

But mainly it's my own cowardly fear that is the jailor,
With my addiction to guilty thoughts, prejudice, phobias,
And simple bad habits.

So Lord, make me free inside,
In my heart and soul and mind and strength,
Free to think clearly, trust wholeheartedly and choose wisely,
Free to love deeply and faithfully,
Free to live simply and positively with gratitude.

With your powerful name break every curse, every bad word,
Every darkness that is set to hinder, harm or confuse me.
With your forgiveness raise my heart to live anew,
And deliver me from bitterness and resentment.
With your living Spirit dwell in me and liberate me
To love enemies and overcome evil with good.

Show me the opportunities today, right here in this small corner
To walk in the freedom of your obedience and goodness,
For your sake, and everyone else's too.
Amen.

Travel Prayer

Lord, a distance lies before me today.
It may only be a few steps from bed to bathroom,
Front door to car or bus, harbour or airport,
But again I must travel, facing both familiar and uncertain,
And I would appreciate your company.

Help me to notice the light, colour and beauty along the way.
Make me laugh and be thankful.
On the dark or dismal stretches give me courage and
compassion.
Make me prayerful.
When I'm adrenaline-pumping excited, or afraid with good
reason,
Keep me safe.
And should I lose my bearings, or stray among thieves,
Rescue me,
For you are my guide, my bodyguard, my friend.

Teach me patience on the road!
Educate me on this journey,
Turn my steps daily into a path of righteousness,
A pilgrimage of trust and creative obedience,
So that journey's end one of these days
Will bring me safe home to your house forever.
Amen.

Songs for the Road

Call it 'pilgrim dissatisfaction'. Godly sorrow perhaps. The blues, or righteous frustration. It creeps up on us over time. Another war or disaster. Another scandal. Another flock of panic stricken victims, seeking a better land.

It's not that we don't feel compassion. It's just that we're tired.

Tired of human wickedness, failure and compromise.

Tired of people suffering and children crying.

Tired of living in a broken world.

Like the author of the 'pilgrim song' Psalm 120 - he feels he's been living 'too long' among deceitful warmongers. He longs for the peace and safety of God's Temple in Jerusalem. He hungers for a sense of God's reassuring presence.

And most probably he senses his own need for atonement.

It's a fact that children of God are never completely 'at home' this side of heaven. But even now we can taste the beginnings of 'eternal life'.

The assurance of sins forgiven through Jesus.

The daily needs met by our generous Father.

Courage, wisdom, patience, joy and love from the Spirit within.

We may not be home quite yet, but every day and every prayer brings us closer. We are by grace pilgrims. We are enroute for God's dwelling.

And so, despite everything,

We sing.

Calvin's Chapel

Travel sometimes gives us the opportunities to brush with 'greatness'. Like seeing the ceiling of the Sistine Chapel or a guitar once played by Jimi Hendrix, or standing on the step where Martin Luther King made his famous 'I have a dream' speech in 1963.

Of course people have many different ideas of what constitutes 'greatness'! Once, while on holiday in Geneva, we worshipped in an English-speaking Church of Scotland service, which was held in 'l'Auditoire de Calvin', a building once central to the Protestant Reformation in Europe. While today's 'Auditoire' has introduced a few modern facilities, much of the original structure has been preserved.

John Calvin and John Knox preached in this very same building in the sixteenth century. Their statues stand along with William Farel and Theodore Beza at 'the Reformation Wall' in the nearby university grounds.

For those of us brought up in a Presbyterian tradition, these men were our spiritual forefathers in faith and practice. Greatly influenced by Calvin, Knox founded the Church of Scotland, with its then-radical form of church government using elected 'Elders'. And seventeenth century Scottish settlers in Ireland brought these new ideas with them and the Presbyterian Church in Ireland was founded.

So yes, there was a sense of being close to something rather great and profound. For us, it was like touching bedrock. A kind of homecoming. Especially when we sang one of the hymns to the Irish tune of 'Be Thou My Vision', one of the pieces sung at my ordination as a minister around twenty-five years ago.

An interesting thing is how modern day Geneva portrays these men and their 'Reformation' as not just a spiritual revival of biblical Christianity, but much more. In their day they helped establish foundational social principles such as education, justice and democracy, on which much of the modern world is based.

On the wall of the Auditoire some of Calvin's inspirational principles are represented. Along with Reformation fundamentals such as 'Grace alone', 'Faith alone' and 'Scripture alone', I was interested to read these:

Fight for solidarity between all people.

Resist evil.

Invent paths of reconciliation.

In other words, John Calvin was not just a formidable theologian; he was a publically-minded pastor, caring for people, desiring everyone's highest good.

I'm reminded of some words of the Apostle Paul, another great theologian/pastor, who urged his first century readers to strive for a godly balance of truth, righteousness and the 'readiness that comes from the gospel of peace.' (Ephesians 6:14, 15) Christians must practise and promote the highest spiritual and moral principles as taught by the Bible, but we must also love and try to live peaceably with those who don't!

Sometimes it is difficult. We may be misunderstood and misrepresented by opponents, but it is the way of our Master, and we are to strive to walk in his light.

And here is something worth considering.

While most of us may never have a following, see our work

in a gallery or museum, or have our statue in the park, we can all move a little closer to greatness every day. We do so when we pray God's will for our lives in Jesus' name, and depend on the Holy Spirit to help us practise the teaching of Scripture.

Like trusting in God's grace for salvation. Seeking to become like Jesus in holy living. And working to build a worldwide community of peace and love.

Crucially, we must do so not for our own fame or fortune but all, as it says on the wall of Calvin's Chapel, 'to the glory of God.'

Community Prayer

Lord, thank you that we are not alone,
For you have placed us here in town and country,
With businesses, services, amenities,
Gardens, roads and fields,
Property, land – and neighbours.

Thank you for the mutual help we can give each other,
For every willing hand or friendly greeting.

Help us to enjoy what you've given us here with gladness,
Thankful and generous to share what we have received.
In our ambitions, save us from selfishness and greed.
May all our efforts benefit others as well as ourselves.
Teach us all to practise courtesy and respect,
Honesty, fair play, patience and kindness.

So grant us to live in safety, and in peace,
As neighbours and friends for the common good.
May those who visit our part of the world
Find a place of prosperity and blessing, and more –
A place of harmony and happiness,
A place of love and of rest.
To your glory.
Amen.

Seasons Prayer

Lord, you are such an artist,
Clothing with majestic colour the late months
When trees shed, and leaves turn and fall,
Paving our way with golden carpets.
You fill our churches with harvest corn and flowers,
And close our days with vast, yearning sunsets,
A benediction of promise.

Thank you for the fireside on the bitter nights,
For the virgin hush of a snowy landscape in the morning,
And that snowdrops blossom in winter,
Another reminder of your faithfulness.

Then, as promised, comes the season of Resurrection,
The ground opens and all lives and grows again.
We are surrounded by new birth,
And lambs play in the fields,
Calling us to celebrate Passover and Easter.

We are released to live in anticipation of summer,
A Sabbath-rest of holiday with the laughter of the redeemed,
Basking in the sunshine of your love and mercy.

Thank you Lord, all year round, for your unfailing kindness,
The seasons of your grace.
Amen.

A Hand

I once knew a doctor who was seriously lacking in 'bedside manner'. Professionally, his colleagues regarded him as one of the finest in his field, but his cold, formal manner often left his patients in tears!

By contrast observe Jesus, sometimes referred to as 'the great physician'. It's not just that he healed people, it's how he did it, with individual care and attention.

'He took her by the hand and said, "My child, get up!"' (Luke 8:54)

As Jairus faces an abyss of inconsolable sorrow, his young daughter having just died, the Lord softly tells him, 'Don't be afraid; just believe, and she will be healed'. Now he could just speak a command as on other occasions, but he chooses to visit the home, giving the parents special courtesy and respect.

Then he takes the young girl's cool hand and gently calls her soul back. She rises, well, and Jesus suggests, perhaps with a smile, that she might like something to eat! (55)

The Son of God offers us his hand, a hand bringing us comfort, reassurance, strong and kind help. Here is a Saviour who is willing to be our friend.

This is the same person who preached about sin and the need for repentance, who challenged the hypocrisy of an uncaring religious establishment with prophetic passion and biting wit (cf. Matthew 23). But with loving devotion and great tenderness, he ministers to individuals and families who humbly seek his help.

Call him God with a human touch. Or the man with a divine touch. My old theology professor used to give us solemn definitions like 'fully God and fully man' which I take to mean God enough to do something and human enough to feel it.

How can we not trust and adore him?

First Stone

He didn't throw it. The first stone. The first one.

He was the only one there who could have, but he chose not to.

Instead he threw out a challenge to the spite-filled crowd, merciless in jealous indignation:

'Let the one with no sin cast the first stone!'

Seething curses, the faithful slunk away, leaving only him, slowly drawing letters in the sand. Him. The one who had no sin.

And of course the accused. The unfaithful.

Me.

He didn't throw that stone. He just looked at me with sad understanding. A look that seemed to say, 'I know … everything. No condemnation, not now, I've got this.'

Then he smiled and helped me to my feet.

'Go in peace,' he said, handing me the stone.

Prayer for Forgiveness

Oh Lord, I'm sorry, I've fouled up.
I've fallen short, missed the mark by a mile,
Crossed the line, entered territory forbidden to me.
I've disobeyed, broken your rules, and my own,
Listened to the wrong voice, given in to the badness in me.
Now I'm broken, compromised, a disgrace,
Slipping backwards into the shadows of guilt and fear.

Can I look again to the one who bought my freedom
With his undeserved suffering?
May I look once more to your cross and live?

I know this is why you came, why you gave yourself,
Yet I am ashamed, embarrassed,
I hate having to confess failure.
So help me to be honest. And humble.
Help me to really turn and change.
I trust in your sacrifice, please forgive me.
Delete my record of shame, let me be clean again,
Considered righteous, and welcome before my Father's
throne.

There's more, I know. This is difficult too but,
Help me forgive those who hurt me so badly.
Let us all live free from bitterness, in love, and in joy, like you.
Amen.

Prayer When Coming to Communion

Lord, thank you for the place you have given me at your table,
And these your beloved with whom I may share
This bread and wine, these precious signs of you.

May we together feel your presence so near, so real,
Humbled in your complete knowledge of us and your absolute holiness,
Enthralled to taste of your deep, self-giving love.

May there be healing in this cup, soul-food in this bread,
Pride-collapsing sweetness in confession and surrender,
And joy in the liberating refilling of your spirit and power.

Help us to celebrate this grace, this salvation, this holy ground,
With deeper gratitude, devotion, obedience,
And the practice of a kind, forgiving fellowship.

Help us to love each other with patience, following your example.
Equip and mobilise us to serve in your Church,
And make public and global the gospel that is you.

You, the God who gave everything, and gives still
That broken, hungry rebels like us might be restored,
Revived and united forever in the sharing of this table.
Amen.

The Lone Ranger

As the movie entered into the elaborate final action sequence, they pulled out all the stops. The familiar trumpet chorus from Rossini's William Tell Overture sounded, the white stallion reared on its hind legs, and we were off at a gallop with the Lone Ranger and Tonto, chasing the baddies through the mountains on a runaway train.

In the theatre, all the men around my age murmured our approval. For a few seconds we were transported back through the years to when we were wee boys watching cartoons on TV. Perched on the arm of the sofa – imagining it as our horse – we urged on the masked rider in the white hat. Hi Ho Silver away!

Now our childhood hero was back, charging fearlessly to the rescue. For just a moment we were assured the innocent would be saved, the villains would get what was coming to them, and good would somehow finally win the day.

A bit like when Jesus rode into Jerusalem on Palm Sunday. Something stirred in the people that day, like an old memory. A prophecy they had been taught as little children, that one day a hero would come to their rescue! So they lined the streets and clapped and cheered, like crowds at a movie premiere, eager for a glimpse, an autograph, a miracle.

But their enthusiasm was short lived, their commitment shallow. Within a week, disillusioned by his insistence on spiritual priorities and holiness, and poisoned by the slander of their leaders, most of them had turned on their Saviour and had him executed.

However, Christians believe this was not a failed mission, nor indeed the end of the story.

The Apostle Paul, writing to the Colossians, insists that Jesus' suffering and death were in fact God's way of bringing us forgiveness, new life and freedom! The witnesses insist Christ rose victorious over death and evil, mighty to save all who trust in him! Alone he has triumphed, and his followers are given to share in the joy of all he has achieved in his cross and Resurrection, for time and eternity!

'Having disarmed the powers and authorities, he made a public spectacle of them, triumphing over them by the cross.' (Colossians 2:15)

Anyone can discover this joy of knowing Jesus through trust and obedient service, even though, like Him, we may temporarily suffer opposition and rejection from some out there in the world.

Being a Christian definitely isn't for wimps. It is for those who want to be heroes. Those who dare to believe, even in the face of all the world's cynicism, that goodness will ultimately be victorious. Those willing to follow in the footsteps of Jesus, the greatest hero of them all!

In the Hills

Lord, thank you for the strength to climb this hill,
For the fine day it is, and the glory of the mountain top.
I love the light, the colour, the clean air, the immensity,
The quietness and being able to see for miles.

Being up here doesn't solve the problems
But it gives me some perspective,
That you see and know all, that there is a big picture,
A purpose to everything that you will somehow bring to pass.

I'm thinking of Abraham on Mount Moriah, Moses on Sinai,
Elijah on Carmel, and yourself on the Mount of Transfiguration,
Moments of revelation and glory, of sacred fear and new trust,
And, though I'm a little hesitant, I'm prompted to pray.

May your presence remain with me as I descend again
To all the things that await my attention,
The sick and demon-oppressed, and the humdrum and
ordinary;
May your glory bring light to our life down there.

Encourage us to remember and think of Mount Calvary
And the atonement provided there.
So, like your people in the Bible,
May we be delivered from idolatry to love your laws,
And walk in your freedom daily.
Amen.

Ray Cross

It is said to be the largest stone cross in Ireland. It stands five and a half metres high, possibly dates from the time of Saint Colmcille (also known as Columba) in the sixth century AD, and can be found in the ruined church of Ray near Falcarragh, Donegal.

It's down a lane, not far off the main road. I've been in the local parish some time now but only heard of it recently. So this rather special and wonderful thing has been there all along, close by, but for ages I've been driving past, oblivious.

And I'm thinking – Jesus, Son of God come in the flesh, Immanuel, God with us, not far away but close by. God is nearer than we realise! But we often just carry on regardless without taking time out to seek his grace or his counsel.

And I'm remembering a couple of instances in the Bible where people had moments of 'Jesus realisation', if I could call it that. As when Simon Peter lets Jesus use his moored boat as an impromptu pulpit and then assists the fishermen in landing a record catch. Suddenly Peter realises this is no ordinary carpenter, that somehow the Almighty has come near, is present in his boat, and fearfully says, 'Go away Lord, I'm a sinful man' (Luke 5:8).

Perhaps the Lord is closer than we think when we are in our workplace. That thought should affect the way we approach our work, and those with whom we work!

The other is when Jesus joins two disciples walking down the road to Emmaus, the evening after he has risen from the dead. Reports are still sketchy, their mood confused and they don't recognise him at first. Not until he joins them for a meal and breaks the bread in their home. Suddenly they realise their crucified master is alive and victorious, that the Almighty has again come near, has visited their place, and their hearts are comforted and thrilled. (cf. Luke 24:30–32)

'No Exit to Hope Street'

It was a long time ago in Belfast during the Troubles.

I was a young student trying to make my way through the city, no mean feat in those days. There were security gates everywhere. Some places you couldn't go, and some places you wouldn't have wanted to go!

The day before had seen another bomb go off near the Europa Hotel. Broken glass was everywhere and people were busy clearing up. Wooden boards had been erected and certain parts of the bus and train stations blocked off. In one place a large sign read, 'No Exit to Hope Street'.

While Hope Street was and remains an actual location, the sign seemed to sum up the mood of those grim days. Sectarian distrust and resentment boiled over into street violence. Against a backdrop of political deadlock, some on both sides committed appalling atrocities. There seemed no end, no way out.

Things are better now. Not perfect, not by a long stretch, but better. We have an ongoing peace process. It's flawed just like the human beings involved in it, but hey, we're a 'work in progress'!

I took my student daughter to Belfast recently.

We drove up and down the Falls and Shankill Roads, past some of the 'flashpoints' where there used to be regular violence. A taxi had stopped by one of the vivid murals on the 'Peace Wall' and the driver was taking a picture of his tourist passengers, to be shared no doubt on social media.

And guess what?

Hope Street was wide open to traffic!

At times our faith in the future can feel fragile enough. Despite all the lessons of history, despite all the noble aspirations of those willing to sacrifice for freedom, peace and justice, human nature seems to keep throwing up fresh generations of small-minded killers. While Belfast appears a little safer on the surface, new ideologies (or old ones in disguise) presently stalk the entire globe prompting new acts of brutality and abuse.

The ancient world was not so different. A succession of empires notched up some truly impressive achievements, art and architecture, but also featured ruthless economic exploitation, slavery and no shortage of murderous tyrants desperate to exert control.

Against that strangely familiar backdrop a little group of Galilean fishermen and former tax collectors made some almost ridiculously optimistic-sounding claims. Such as finding real motivation and courage in the real love and grace of a real God. Or finding fulfilment in simple lifestyle and brotherly love rather than endless material gain. Or almost cheerful trust in the face of suffering and death, believing the best is yet to come with heavenly resurrection.

One of them, Simon Peter, puts it far better than me:

'Praise be to the God and Father of our Lord Jesus Christ! In His great mercy He has given us new birth into a living hope, and into an inheritance that can never perish, spoil or fade, kept in heaven for you ...' (1 Peter 1:3–9).

Jesus Christ has risen victorious over death and evil. So neither the pathetic, wicked acts of humans or the evil powers that inspire them are the end of the story. People of faith can find comfort looking forward to a heavenly inheritance with Jesus.

We're not perfect yet but hey, sanctification is another 'work in progress'. Sometimes we limp a little in the short term. Sometimes our wounds still hurt.

But since Easter, Hope Street has been reopened.

Permanently.

Easter Prayer

Thank you Lord, for now we know for sure
That anything is possible.
The eternal can taste death, and humanity rise everlasting.
Your cross and empty tomb are the final word,
The conclusive statement that declares hope and freedom.
Anything is possible. Everything opens to us.

Here in your grace we stand, children of the Resurrection,
Cleansed by your sacrifice, reborn in your Spirit,
Destined for your glory and commissioned for your service.
Believers. Followers of the crucified but living one,
Given to share your victory celebration and authority.

Those around us don't get it, can't see it, they just see
An institution past the sell-by-date, beneath contempt or pity.
Forgive us if we have lived as such!

Let today be a day of revival for Resurrection perspective!
Into our darkest corners shine your light of hope!
Help us view our current sorrows in the context of everlasting
life!
Make your joy our strength, and our song compelling,
An invitation to all to come, taste and see
This Living Bread, our living Lord is good, so good!
Blessed be your name!
Amen.

Ascension Prayer

Lord, it's your lap of honour, your time on the winner's stand.
You have contended, you have conquered,
And now are crowned undisputed Champion!

We are sharing your glory, punching the air in victory,
Cheering, waving our arms in wild, joyful celebration.
Our hero, now you reign, and always will.

We want to chant your name to the grandstands,
Show them the replay again and again.
We will wear your team colours with pride!

So please Lord, autograph the programme of our lives!
Mark and own us as yours, take us as your supporters.
Put the Spirit of you deep in our hearts.

Speak with your all—unique authority and make things happen,
In us, in everyone, in all things.
Expose the enemy for the cruel cheats they always were,
And empower your people for worldwide jubilation!

For yours *are* the power and the glory, the eternal kingdom.

Amen.

Against the Wind

I was looking out the study window one day and this goose was flapping like fury but getting nowhere. He was flying into the wind against what seemed like a proverbial brick wall. For all his effort he was staying in the one place, zero progress.

And I'm sitting there thinking, why doesn't he just turn around?

I mean Scandinavia must be nice this time of year. Why does it always have to be Greenland? From where I was sitting, Sweden looked the more attractive option. Certainly the easier journey! Of course Mr Goose probably doesn't realise he has options. He's just sticking to his practised route.

Like the Pharisees in Jesus' day. The Gospels contain numerous episodes, like Luke 6:6–11, where Jesus did something wonderful and God-honouring, but the religious establishment immediately discussed how they might get rid of him because it didn't fit with their idea of Sabbath observance!

They were zealously defending the traditions handed down by their forefathers, oblivious, or perhaps in truth wilfully blind to the fact that the Spirit of God was blowing in a new direction.

So they couldn't or wouldn't see the real, dynamic presence of God in the words and actions of Jesus of Nazareth.

It seems to be a thing with some religious people. Defend orthodoxy at all costs, even if actual, interactive faith died a long time ago. Flap till you drop and get nowhere!

Wouldn't it be better if we turned and went with the Spirit's flow, letting Him show us some new territory? Same Jesus, but fresh and alive, challenging, motivating, heart-renewing, soul-transforming and r-e-a-l.

Let the other birds think what they like. This direction takes us places, the wind of God empowering us to do his will like never before.

You coming?

Pentecost Prayer

Lord, I hear the wind racing in the chimney,
The coal and turf flicker in the hearth, flames bright.
Glad to be inside, I pray for your Spirit to come,
To invade my heart with a burning purity and fresh rushing power,
That I might rest secure this night as a child of God,
And go forth in the new day equipped as a fruitful witness.

Lord, thank you for the pictures and promises of your Word,
The bubbling spring of living water, the gallons of top-class wine,
The living, heaven-sent Gift to be poured out abundantly,
That those who hunger and thirst for righteousness may be filled,
And your church be a force for good on Earth.

So yes, Lord, pour out your Spirit on your people here!
Fill our souls to overflowing with the wonders of Christ,
The always dependable grace, the deep and precious love,
Reclaiming, redeeming, renewing, replenishing, reviving.
Fill us with a common heart and purpose, that with all our various gifts,
We might become a united and ever-growing fellowship,
One people of peace, one body, yours!
For your glory!
Amen.

The Golden Gate

It was the last day of our holiday. The girls were taking an open top bus tour of San Francisco so I did what any sensible man on holiday in a large American city would do.

I rented a Harley Davidson motorcycle. A 1340cc Heritage Softail to be precise, I edged out into the traffic listening to that distinctive throaty rumble from the exhaust.

I tried to remember the directions I'd been given, two blocks then right, right again and straight on Van Ness. Once I hit the '101' I knew I'd be okay. By now I was in the thick of a multi-lane street cutting through the city block by block, surrounded by people from every imaginable ethnic background, driving cars, vans or even huge lorries. We skirted the borders of areas like Tenderloin and Chinatown.

Suddenly, overhead I saw a sign, a welcome confirmation that I was headed the right way: 'Route 101 – All lanes lead to Golden Gate'.

And sure enough, within minutes I saw it rising out of the mist up ahead, the iconic Golden Gate Bridge. It was hard to suppress a chuckle as I opened the throttle and roared across to explore the sunshine of the beautiful Sonoma Valley.

Now here's a thought: when we're on the right road, we may meet different people in different lanes, with different vehicles but we're all headed the same way. Our destination is the same, the Golden Gate, and all the opportunity that lies beyond. God doesn't make it difficult, quite the opposite. He gave his own Son that people of all backgrounds could get their lives on course.

Christians have different temperaments and styles and operate through different denominations, but we all share one Lord and Saviour. Following our Master Jesus brings us together on the same path, and leads to the same conclusion, the glory of eternal life.

We are given to share the fellowship of this 'journey'. Therefore, just as it says in the Highway Code, a little mutual courtesy and consideration is always in order!

Jesus urged His listeners to get off the sinful road leading to destruction and find their course in Him, trusting and obeying the One Who loves and gave Himself for us. (Matthew 7:13–14)

Then, by His grace, we all shall one day arrive safe and sound at the 'Golden Gate' of Heaven!

Church Prayer

Lord, thank you for this place, with its atmosphere and memories,
For the tunes old and new that stir the blood,
And raise our voices and souls to you.
Thank you for scripture in language we can understand,
And that we may come together to a house of prayer.

Thank you for the people, your Body, our family,
Yet here is where it can be so disappointing.
We confess our smallmindedness,
Our lack of fervour, of holiness, of love!
Too often we have broken your Body,
And crippled our witness with our infighting.
What a pale shadow we must be of all that you desire!

Forgive us Lord, and renew us in your likeness.
Create clean, fresh, joyful hearts in us that delight in your will.
Fill us with your Spirit and overflowing love,
For each other, and for all people.
Build your kingdom here, in us, among us, through us.

That we might be a bride worthy of your delight,
That your people might be your house, filled with light and welcome,
Everywhere.
Amen.

Homeplace

Home is the city my people no longer inhabit, and the places
I have yet to dwell,
It's the kind, unpretty tree in a strange town, under which I'm
sheltering to eat lunch.
Home is where I left yesterday, where I shall return tomorrow
and
It's the place I am right now, all I shall be and do and see today,
For it is within me, the whole unseen plan, enriching my soul
as it unfolds.

It's that familiar place where my flowers are planted and our
children grow,
Where I park my car at night, kick off shoes and softly play
guitar.
It is the warmth of our bed, the mutual help, the space of
understanding.
Home is the hallowed ground of love, secure among the
everyday chores.
It is the beautiful gift, the sweet heritage of all that is shared.

Home is waiting there yet may be found anywhere,
At work or worship or in some far-off, unexpected pleasure.
If home is where our hearts lie, mine sleeps far and wide,
For time and again home has come to me in every place,
Shown by family and friends in blessed hospitality.

Behind the unnecessary kindness of strangers and faithful
Remembrance of distant friends I imagine the strong

Quiet presence of angels, touching my life with wisdom,
Humbling my foolish ego, enlarging my worldworn heart
With love renewed, a homeplace beating inside.

Home is the open road that connects our towns and hearts,
Our histories and futures, our tears of sorrow, thanks and hope.
It's the kettle and easy chair that assure perpetual welcome.
It's going away to find where you belong, and returning content,
At peace and comfortable, at home in your own skin.

Solitude Prayer

Lord, I'm on my own just now,
And I really don't want to stray and fall
In loneliness and self-pity.
Therefore I'm repeating with extra earnestness
My frequent invitation: please be with me.

Inhabit my body and mind and take authority here.
May the cold and dark not win in me but be crushed
And banished by the comforting light of your presence.

Refresh my soul with thoughts from your truth-filled Word —
Wise counsel, faithful direction, loving promise.
Inspire me with new enthusiasm for the wonder of your
creation,
The assuring of your cleansing grace and liberating power,
The delegated joy of being commissioned as your servant.

May this time of reflection help me think more clearly and
constructively.
May the quietness be my opportunity to pray with more
focus and passion.
May the unhurried stillness foster peace and strength in my
soul
Live in me so that I may know that those who trust in you
Are never alone.
Ever.
Amen.

Morning Prayer

Lord, it's morning and I'm awake. Thank you!
For bringing me safe through the dark of night
To rise and share the light of this new day,
That I can open my eyes and see,
Stand up, walk and go places,
Talk and enjoy relationship –

Another opportunity to celebrate the life you give,
To glorify you and enjoy you forever!

Let me not squander this day in selfish complaining,
Or wasteful inactivity, but rejoice
In more chances to savour the beauty and gladness
Of all the good things you so generously provide.
Help me overcome my natural fears and hesitation
To discover new ways of serving and showing kindness,
New challenges of love and mercy,
New avenues of blessing for us all.

I'm remembering our master rose from death early in the
morning,
So I'm praying – Raise me up from a dead, lesser way of living
To a more determined hope today.
Live in my thoughts, prayers, words and actions.
Be glorified in me,
Today.
Amen.

Small Corners

It wasn't the prettiest corner of the property.

Just a bank of rough, brown earth, with a couple of tree stumps and no shortage of weeds, at the foot of a wall built with bare grey blocks. Hardly an exhibit for a flower show!

But it is fairly sheltered and it does get the sun so I thought, why not?

My gardening knowledge and skills are fairly limited, but I've enjoyed having a go. I pulled out the weeds, dug the earth over with a hoe and planted a few flowering shrubs. I added some pots with larger bushes, and nailed up a wooden trellis to dress the wall a bit. A lick of paint and a hanging basket helped take the bare look off it.

Maybe still not a prizewinner, but slowly I think we're getting somewhere. I was really quite chuffed when the kids got me a plaque to hang on the wall which reads, 'Dad's Garden'!

And I think perhaps I'm beginning to realise a little of why the first job the Creator entrusted to mankind was to tend a garden. Genesis 1:31 tells us, 'God saw all that He had made, and it was very good.' It feels good to have your hands in the earth, gently planting living things, faithfully watering them, and of course having the pleasure of watching them grow and flourish and blossom. It's more joy than work!

Of course there are challenges. Some days the wind blows leaves and rubbish into my little patch. Sometimes the dog insists on pawing all over it. It needs a little love and protection, but I think it's worth it.

And I'm thinking, maybe it's a sort of picture of what we're meant to do with our lives generally. Whatever we've been given — we should treasure it, nurture it, look after it and make it as beautiful as we can, with thanks and reverence for the one who gives us all we are and have. As we care for our present environment, we prepare for the glory that will be revealed in the resurrection age when destructive exploitation and pollution will be no more, and creation is restored to wholeness.

I'm reminded of an old children's hymn which includes the lines:

'Jesus bids us shine first of all for Him...

You in your small corner, and I in mine.'

Whatever 'corner' you've been given to inhabit and tend today, large or small, do everything you can, with words and acts of kindness and love, to make it beautiful!

Lifted up in Music

Lord, it plays – orchestra, band, solo, whatever
And takes us to another place.
The swell and soar, the riff, the plaintive air,
The voice or chorus, some unforgettable melody
And we're lifted almost out of ourselves.
We laugh, clap, tap, dance, hearts enlarged,
Hair on end and tears in our eyes.
Dear sweet Lord, thank you for the gift of music!

Hear, oh Lord, the cry of the heart in sorrow or delight.
Listen to the unspoken prayer.
Bring peace to the players and the hearers,
Harmony to the souls of the gathering,
And sweetness to our living,
Even when the song is ended.

Be our Songwriter, Conductor, Mentor, Band-Leader.
Make of us something inspiring,
A symphony of praise, hope, faith reborn,
And love, all-conquering love!
Let the music of your good news of grace
Dwell in us richly today!
Amen.

Sunshine of His Love

Solar energy – now there's a thing.

My wife bought me a gift, a bunch of small, solar-powered lamps. You'd hardly notice them during the day, but look out into the garden around bedtime and there they are, shining brightly with a clear, white glow. I don't have to switch them on, they seem to know what to do each evening all on their own.

Cleverly-designed, they soak up the sun's rays during the hours of natural daylight so they can illuminate the garden in the dark. The more sunshine they get, the brighter and longer the glow!

They teach me a simple lesson. Jesus claimed to be 'the Light of the world' (John 8:12), and urges his followers to reflect his light of grace and truth and love, saying, 'You are the light of the world ... people [don't] light a lamp and put it under a bowl ... Let your light shine before men, that they may see your good deeds and praise your Father in heaven.' (Matthew 5:14–16)

There's no question of the 'darkness' around us – poverty, abuse, hopelessness in the face of wars and environmental crises to mention just a few. Modestly, but unashamedly, by our actions of kindness and mercy and faithful words of 'good news', Christians are called to reflect the light and hope of Jesus' rescuing love. And here's where my little solar lamps come in ...

The more time we prayerfully spend in the sunshine of his loving presence, the brighter we will shine!

A Storm Came Last Night

Yesterday had been fine, a calm day, then suddenly last evening there it was. The wind. It caught me unawares as I left a house where I was visiting, almost causing me to lose balance. Through the night I could feel it buffeting the gable of the house. Where we live overlooks Horn Head and Sheephaven Bay in North Donegal, and this morning I'm watching the clouds being driven across the sky and the shrubs in the garden almost bending over double.

And I'm thinking about a man who came to see Jesus.

Nicodemus was a bit confused but intrigued by Jesus, not sure whether to feel threatened or thrilled. So he came to find out more, cautiously at first, in the quietness and privacy of evening. (cf. John 3)

Things were happening in the neighbourhood, in his own head and heart, that were making him think of the God he read about in the Old Testament days of Moses. This man Jesus was preaching with authority like a prophet, and backing his words up with jaw-dropping miracles. Crowds were following him but other religious leaders were plotting to kill him. What was it all about?

So Jesus spoke about the wind.

We can't see it. We may not be able to completely understand or explain it. But it's real. And it's powerful. A storm brews as it sends clouds rushing and brings the world to its knees.

God was at work in the neighbourhood. His Son had come in the flesh and when He was 'lifted up' on the cross in sacrifice He would provide redemption for the world. As the Holy Spirit of God worked invisibly, people were finding power from beyond themselves to change and make a new start. A new beginning inside. A new birth.

And although Nicodemus seems to have been confused initially, the fact that he could perceive what his fellow Pharisees couldn't, and that he came to Jesus suggests that a 'new birth' was starting to happen in him. Later in John's Gospel it's interesting to see that Nicodemus came to Pilate with Joseph of Arimathea to request permission to give Jesus a decent burial. By that stage he was not afraid to be identified as a follower of Jesus. The 'wind' of God's Spirit was obviously still blowing in his heart and life!

The last time it was this stormy here most people were staying indoors or running for cover, but I noticed two intrepid windsurfers in their wetsuits, jumping waves out in the bay.

I guess a lot of people are cautious about genuine interaction with God, afraid of whipping up a storm they can't control. But for those who perceive and welcome the work of His Spirit, who let Him clear the clouds of sin and fear and cause us to bow to Jesus as Lord – the life and adventure are just beginning!

Evening Prayer

Lord, the hours on the clock are getting shorter, night is closing in.
Some are ready for bed while others are only waking up!
I'm remembering those verses which tell me
That darkness is as light to you. If so, then
Help me live these next hours transparently and without fear.

Join me. Be my reassuring companion, my protection,
My wisdom at the party, my rock on which to dance.
Guide my thoughts, words and actions this evening,
That I and those around me can enjoy with respect.

Later bring me home safe to the comfort of familiar surroundings
And kind words with those I love.
Gift us all with peaceful hearts and refreshing sleep.

And as I lie down and drift beyond conscious self-control,
I commit to you my dreams,
That even there you would guard me from things dishonourable,
And feed my soul with promises of things faithful, inspirational,
And visions of all you make possible.

Lord, I surrender myself to your care tonight,
And smile to remember –
My Defender never sleeps.
Amen.

Yosemite

It really didn't look that hopeful.

We'd been urged to make the arduous, twisty drive up to 'Glacier Point' which, we were assured, was a stargazer's dream. With little or no artificial light, the heavens would be bright with thousands of stars.

But things had dulled down as the day went by and the evening was overcast. In fairness, the panoramic sweep of mountains from the viewpoint was still majestic but, well, a little grey. We even felt a 'spit' of rain and wondered about heading back down. But others had gathered, and seemed to be waiting in anticipation and so we hung about.

Then, just about ten minutes before eight, the sun appeared momentarily, below the clouds and just above the western horizon. Suddenly the valley was filled with fresh light and the mountains were bathed in a warm glow. People gasped in wonder and cameras started clicking. As if that weren't enough, after the sun actually sank beneath the distant rim, the sky took on a range of amazing colours, red, purple, and blue, in what they told us was an 'alpine glow', and the distant mountain peaks shimmered in pink.

It was awesome!

We didn't see many stars that night, but what we did see was more spectacular than we could have imagined. It wasn't what we'd expected but we were in no way disappointed!

And maybe there is a lesson here in faith. Faith is not demanding the heavens to give us what we think we want, but waiting to see, and accepting with gratitude what the heavens choose to give.

Jesus Christ taught His followers to seek God's kingdom and will before our own ambitions, praying to the Creator and Ruler, 'Your will be done on earth (in my life, in our community) as it is in Heaven!'

The Psalmist writes: 'I wait for the Lord, my soul waits, and in His word I put my hope.' (Psalm 130:5)

As we look to the future we may feel eager to grab opportunities which appear to be beckoning, or daunted by those looming challenges, or perhaps a bit of both! But encouraged by God's Word and His Son, the Rescuer Who came from heaven, we might say with A W Tozer:

'We may safely preach a friendly heaven.'!

Under the Stars

Lord, the road is twisty and dark, its edges unclear,
A stone wall or hedgerow perhaps, I'm not sure.
But the clouds are clearing, I can see stars,
Pleiades and Orion, like old friends smiling a greeting.
I spot the Great Bear and the Pole Star
And walk on with renewed confidence
Now I know which way is home.

I praise and thank you who made the starry host
And have come down to be my rescuer and guide.
I sense the rod and staff of the Good Shepherd
And know that I need fear no evil now.

Comforted by you, I am learning to trust, to ask, so –
Guide me Lord, in the decisions I must make this week, this
year,
About study, work, friends, enemies,
Times, places, ideas, opportunities,
Things I love, hate, welcome or dread!

More, lift my eyes and thoughts above my own little world
To see and share your universal heart for your creation.
Lead me in paths of righteousness, truth and compassion.
Fire in me zeal like yours, to live in your will and pray without
ceasing,
That all may discover your saving, leading light.
Amen.

Alone in the Sanctuary

Lord, it's just me this time, no congregation, no crowd.
I'm here on my own, I just need a minute,
To be near your altar, to bow my head, to refocus.

Just me and a few candles of faith, and the massive stillness.

I know I have nothing to fear in my Father's house.
And I know your presence will go with me when I leave.
And it's ok, you don't have to say anything.

Just let me shelter beneath your cross,
And consider my burdens here, by your wounded side.
Help me view things in the pure light of your resurrection,
And stand in a place of grace by the power of your Spirit.
Thus may I rest for this moment, this lifetime
In the loving shadow of the Almighty.

Thank you Lord. I'm alright now.
I'm good to go.
Amen.